Library Technology
REPORTS
Expert Guides to Library Systems and Services

Micro-credentials and Digital Badges

Edited by Emily Rimland and Victoria Raish

ALA TechSource
alatechsource.org

American Library Association

Library Technology
REPORTS

ALA TechSource purchases fund advocacy, awareness, and accreditation programs for library professionals worldwide.

Volume 55, Number 3

Micro-credentials and Digital Badges

ISBN: 978-0-8389-1816-6

American Library Association

50 East Huron St.
Chicago, IL 60611-2795 USA
alatechsource.org
800-545-2433, ext. 4299
312-944-6780
312-280-5275 (fax)

Advertising Representative

Samantha Imburgia
simburgia@ala.org
312-280-3244

Editor

Samantha Imburgia
simburgia@ala.org
312-280-3244

Copy Editor

Judith Lauber

Production

ALA Production Services

Editorial Assistant

Colton Ursiny

Cover Design

Alejandra Diaz

Library Technology Reports (ISSN 0024-2586) is published eight times a year (January, March, April, June, July, September, October, and December) by American Library Association, 50 E. Huron St., Chicago, IL 60611. It is managed by ALA TechSource, a unit of the publishing department of ALA. Periodical postage paid at Chicago, Illinois, and at additional mailing offices. POSTMASTER: Send address changes to Library Technology Reports, 50 E. Huron St., Chicago, IL 60611.

ALA TechSource

alatechsource.org

About the Editors

Emily Rimland is an Information Literacy Librarian and Learning Technologies Coordinator at Penn State. She enjoys providing instruction, reference, and outreach services to undergraduate students and holds an MLIS from the University of Pittsburgh. Her research interests include pedagogical innovation and effective learning methodologies, the application of emerging technologies to library services, and instructional technologies. She was the founder of the ACRL Digital Badge Interest Group and was a Teaching and Learning with Technology Faculty Fellow at Penn State. She received the 2018 Library Instruction Round Table Librarian Recognition Award.

Victoria Raish is the Online Learning Librarian for Penn State University. She received her PhD in learning, design, and technology from Penn State and her MAT from the University of Southern California. She has worked extensively with digital badges in a variety of settings, including information literacy and STEM teacher professional development. She has also presented at ACRL on digital badges and published in *College and Research Libraries*. Her current work involves using digital badges in introducing online students to the library and increasing information literacy instruction for online students. Her other research interests are systemic change, educational technology, and the student experience in online learning. The library digital badges at Penn State created with Emily Rimland have received national media attention.

Abstract

Digital badges, a type of micro-credential, have been heralded for the last five years as a key trend in education to provide competency-based pathways to learning. Micro-credentials allow for a unique way to teach students information literacy skills. Many libraries may be interested in implementing a micro-credentialing program but may have questions about design, mechanics, and sustainability. This report will give readers much of that background information. After reviewing the report, readers should be able to

- define micro-credentials and the mechanics of using them
- identify learning scenarios where micro-credentials can be beneficial
- acknowledge the design considerations that are specific to badges
- identify partnerships needed for a successful program
- know the existing systems possible for building a micro-credentialing program for information literacy or library skills
- feel empowered with knowledge to begin building a program

Subscriptions

alatechsource.org/subscribe

Contents

Contents, continued

Chapter 1

Introduction

Emily Rimland and Victoria Raish

Could a one dollar bill ever be more valuable than a one hundred dollar bill? Surprisingly, yes. Imagine walking up to a vending machine that takes only one dollar bills, but all you have is a one hundred dollar bill. Sometimes a smaller item of currency is actually more valuable than a larger one, depending on the context.

Similarly, think about academic credentials. Degrees and professional certifications are extremely valuable, but in some scenarios, it could be more important to showcase specific skills. This is where micro-credentials and digital badges can be helpful and are thus seeing a rise as a new form of educational currency. Technically speaking, digital badges are a subtype of micro-credential, but for the purposes of this report, we will use these terms interchangeably. Micro-credentials are a virtual, portable way of cashing in on acquired learning, especially granular skills. And being able to articulate your specific skills could be the determining factor in landing the job, getting the promotion, or earning the grade.

Information literacy is a skill that is particularly well-suited for micro-credentialing. Our foray into micro-credentials started in 2012, after Emily attended a local conference session about digital badges. Around the same time, Educause published one of its *7 Things to Know About . . .* series about digital badges.[1] Having taught information literacy skills for years in the "one shot" format, we immediately felt that micro-credentials seemed to be a way to extend the librarian's reach outside the short time available in a face-to-face, one-time session. Plus, in most degree programs, information literacy is not a separately recognized skill, and yet employers, instructors, and others agree it is an important skill. To verify our suspicions, we conducted a nationwide survey of employers in various industries and reaffirmed that information literacy was an important skill for graduates entering the workplace. We also learned about employers' nascent attitudes to digital badges.[2] We then built a scaffolded information literacy digital badge program from the ground up based on our findings, also using other sources such as the ACRL *Information Literacy Competency Standards for Higher Education* and the *Framework for Information Literacy for Higher Education*. The primary purpose of our program is to use the information literacy badges within general education courses. For example, a student may be required or recommended to use a chosen badge within an English class. In the fall 2018 semester alone, we had more than 1,500 students earn one of our information literacy or "orientation level" badges, and we worked with thirty-three sections of general education courses at Penn State to implement the badges in the courses.

At this scale, the implementation of micro-credentials has truly changed the conversation about information literacy instruction in many positive ways. But no matter the scale, there is much to gain from implementing a digital badge program. One of the biggest benefits has been what Carla Casilli referred to as "self-reflexivity where the builders learned as much about themselves as the earners did."[3] Our insight into a learner's thinking echoes what Casilli said and has been a surprising and rewarding piece of evaluating student work via digital badges.

This report will provide information about the past, present, and future of digital badges on a broad scale as well as within libraries. It will discuss other aspects to consider when building a digital badge program, including instructional design, deployment considerations, assessment, and partnerships. We hope that this issue of *Library Technology Reports* will illuminate some of the benefits of using micro-credentials so that you feel empowered to try them as part of your programming or instruction.

Notes

1. Educause Learning Institute, "7 Things You Should Know about Badges," *7 Things You Should Know About . . .*, June 2012, https://library.educause.edu/resources/2012/6/7-things-you-should-know-about-badges.
2. Victoria Raish and Emily Rimland, "Employer Perceptions of Critical Information Literacy Skills and Digital Badges," *College and Research Libraries* 77, no. 1 (2016): 87–113, https://doi.org/10.5860/crl.77.1.87.
3. Carla Casilli, "Foreword," in *Teaching with Digital Badges: Best Practices for Libraries*, ed. Kelsey O'Brien and Trudi E. Jacobson (Lanham, MD: Rowman and Littlefield, 2018), xi.

Chapter 2

Overview, Definitions, and Benefits

Emily Rimland and Victoria Raish

Digital badges or micro-credentials are virtual representations of a skill or knowledge, typically a granular one. They can often be "stacked" or combined to paint a picture of a learner's unique skills or add up to a larger certificate (see figure 2.1). Digital badges specifically include a visual representation—a virtual token or icon that is clickable. By clicking on the badge, you can see various metadata about what the learner did to earn the badge (see figure 2.2). Badges are often earned on badging platforms that allow users to also collect and showcase their badges, and the badges are often verified in different ways by a person or institution. Because badges are stackable or combinable into a "learning constellation," badge designers often build them in a hierarchy or pathway to make earning them flexible and customizable. In the same way curricula use traditional credentials, most curricula can be "badged." The tricky part is making the learning meaningful and impactful; however, meaning and impact can be incorporated when design and deployment are considered up front. Badges can also be offered for all levels, from beginning to advanced, and all disciplines and areas of study, from medicine to project management to information technology to manufacturing.

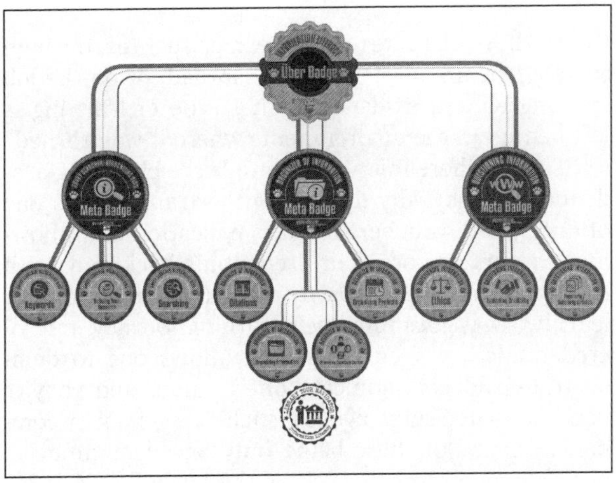

Figure 2.1
The hierarchy of Penn State's Information Literacy digital badges. The badges shown at the bottom are to be earned first and are grouped by category of skill. If a learner earns all the badges in a category, they can earn a meta badge. If the three meta badges are earned, they can earn the uber badge.

The oft-used comparison to Girl Scout or Boy Scout badges as the analog equivalent of digital badges is accurate, albeit hackneyed, but it doesn't tell the entire story. Another way to think about digital badges is using the paper receipt analogy. When you buy something in a store, you walk away with a piece of paper showing what you bought. This official document proves that you paid for an item and that it is yours should you need to return it, get a rebate, or make another transaction. However, store receipts often use a cryptic language of abbreviations for each item and communicate only the bare essentials. Similarly, the college transcript is the checkout receipt of the academic world. The transcript is the "receipt" students often need as "proof of purchase" when applying for graduate school or other opportunities. It lists courses, credits, and grades; however, the typical transcript doesn't provide any depth or nuance about what a student learned in each course. The transcript may not even explain the abbreviations for the courses listed, leaving one to guess what they mean, not to mention what was learned. Transcripts also do not typically recognize learning that happens outside

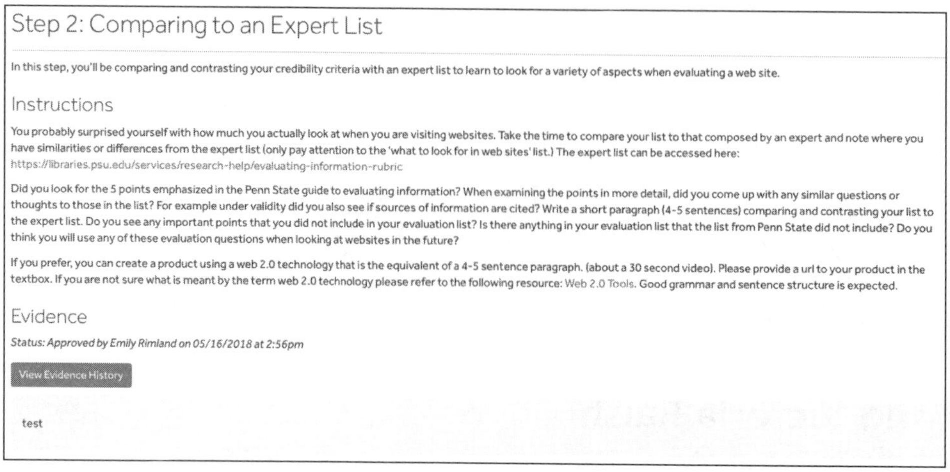

Figure 2.2
An example of the metadata for a step completed to earn a badge. This image shows the instructions, the evidence submitted to earn approval for the step (in this case a test response was used for demonstration purposes), and when and who approved the work.

the traditional routes of seat time, such as through service-learning projects, study abroad, or on-the-job training. Often, evidence of that type of learning is left behind in the environments where it was earned.

This is where micro-credentials are changing academic currency—by disrupting the transcript as one of only a few vouchers of one's education and allowing learners to port their credentials back and forth between schools and jobs. By recognizing the granular learning that goes into one's learning journey, micro-credentials are a currency that allows one to demonstrate and communicate one's value, and they're backed by an issuing agency, such as a school or company. Instead of there being only one denomination of academic currency, such as the bachelor's degree, micro-credentials allow recognition for learning that doesn't replace a degree but positively augments it.

Going digital with credentials allows for many benefits, and below we'll outline some of them. For some of the drawbacks, see chapter 4.

One of benefits is data richness. The digital nature of badges allows the capturing of various details that encourage and support assessment, validity, security, and analysis. In a time when data insight platforms and learning analytics are changing higher education by providing a wealth of data that can be used to help students succeed, badges too have their place. The steps taken to earn a badge, along with a student's evidence for each step, provide a way to assess learning because the evaluator is seeing the evidence and judging whether or not it passes muster. Additionally, on most badging platforms, detailed information about learners' progress either on a personal level or in the aggregate can be easily found. Detailed information, such as the number of steps completed, badges earned, and dates earned, can be conveyed by reports easily generated by badging platforms. In terms of validity and security, most badging platforms can be tied to a type of authentication to verify the identity of the learner by having learners log in via an institution's authentication system. Many institutions use official brands or marks on the badge icon itself as a way of indicating the issuer's validity. Third-party services can be employed to research and verify the validity of a badge. No doubt blockchain technology, which is rising in use, will be used in the future to completely authenticate the veracity of a badge and the earner's identity.

Micro-credentials also offer social benefits. One way they do so is through increasing equity and access to education. Micro-credentials allow a learner to recognize parts of a degree such as specific courses or skills; thus, learners can display proof of learning and skills even if they don't have a full degree yet. For example, if you earn three-quarters of a degree and have to delay completing your degree due to a family emergency, you still incur three-quarters of the debt for the degree but don't have much proof to show for it. If you have micro-credentials, you at least have something to show for your learning other than debt. Additionally, when you are able to resume your studies, you have a clearer picture of what you did and where you need to go to resume your learning. Micro-credentials also support the belief that learners should own their academic records. Because of the nature of micro-credentials, learners have more autonomy to port their records back and forth to different institutions or jobs.

Clearly, micro-credentials have many potential benefits; a few are listed above, and many more will be outlined in following chapters. However, in order for micro-credentials to reach a tipping point for adoption, many groups need to play a role and coordinate the different aspects of badging, both technologically and systemically, for badges to gain ground. Libraries can be a major player in this orchestration moving forward, and in the following chapters, we'll share strategies for how you can get involved.

Chapter 3

The Badge Ecosystem

Emily Rimland and Victoria Raish

Like many things virtual, digital credentials came into existence with the rise in popularity of the internet.[1] Paper certificates for courses taken or skills learned were and are a recognized form of academic credential. Thus it wasn't a big leap to make them digital, especially with the rise in online learning that started in the 1990s. Badges also have a gamification component, as they allow learners to work toward a goal and "level up" their learning, which helps boost engagement and learning.

Early in the history of digital credentials, there was a concerted effort to make digital badges a type of open credential. An open credential is one that adheres to a technical specification in order to ensure a structure that is uniform and universal no matter where it comes from or who issues it. By agreeing to use an open standard called the Open Badge Infrastructure (OBI), creators of digital badges ensured that all digital badges are interoperable with different platforms or systems regardless of who issued them or where they were earned.[2] Use of the open standard also means that digital badges from different places can be collected and packaged so that learners can showcase their skills in ways that fit the needs of the situation. Earners of badges can share them in social media venues but also have the option to display them in a virtual backpack, with Mozilla's being the first and best-known container for digital badges. Mozilla (yes, the organization that also makes the Firefox browser) created open badges and the virtual backpack in 2011 with funding from the MacArthur Foundation.[3] Since 2017, the open badge standard has been maintained by IMS Global Learning Consortium, which is one purveyor of educational technology standards. In early 2018, the Open Badge 2.0 standard was released and added necessary updates.

The OBI also allows for a wealth of metadata to be included along with the badge. It is this aspect that makes digital credentials game changers and unique when compared to other credentials. Some examples of the metadata included in an open badge are

- who issued the badge (by name or institution)
- who earned the badge
- when the badge was earned (Badges can also be set to expire after a set period of time.)
- details about the work that was required of the learner to earn the badge
- alignment of the badge work with outcomes, standards, or frameworks
- the actual work, that is, the evidence the learner submitted to earn the badge

This last bullet point is perhaps the most important because now the work that the student has done can be vetted, verified, and assessed by others, such as an employer who is evaluating a job applicant's claims about a skill.

Badging Platforms

The people and organizations (Mozilla, MacArthur Foundation, Gates Foundation, etc.) that created and implemented the OBI did a remarkable amount of work that focused on innovation and openness, which in turn motivated others to get involved in digital credentialing. Changes in higher education also helped to drive adoption of new education technology and credentialing systems (more on this later in the chapter). With an open standard and broader adoption came the rise of more badging platforms to take advantage of these developments. Badging platforms are where learners go to find and earn badges and to curate any badges they've earned. Vendors of badging platforms seek to provide different features or designs to make them more user-friendly, accessible, and robust, but all are built around the OBI so that badges that are output from that system are interoperable with other systems. Badge Wiki keeps a list of platforms that are available along with some details of each. Badge platforms, like other web-based applications, are a bit of a moving target because, as with many other kinds of businesses, companies buy each other or merge. Until recently, the three major platforms were Credly, Acclaim, and Badgr; however, with Credly purchasing Acclaim (owned by Pearson) in 2018, that list is now down to two major players. Still, there are many smaller platforms, even a number of homegrown, institution-specific platforms. For example, at our institution (Penn State), a badging platform was developed in-house after a small group received seed funding for innovative projects, and we've used this system for many years with much success.

Badge Wiki
https://badge.wiki

Credly
https://info.credly.com

Badgr
https://badgr.com

Penn State Digital Badges Platform
https://badgesapp.psu.edu

LMSs and LTI

Along with badging platforms, new ways to use and integrate digital badges continue to develop. One major area of development is tied to learning management systems (LMSs). LMSs (also known as course management systems, or CMSs) are online applications that "[provide] an instructor with a set of tools and a framework that allows the relatively easy creation of online course content and the subsequently teaching and management of that course including various interactions with students taking the course."[4] Some popular LMSs at the time of publication are Canvas, Moodle, Desire2Learn, edX, and Blackboard. LMSs have changed the way courses are delivered to students in both face-to-face and online learning and in institutions from grade schools on up through postsecondary. This change is felt so much that the LMS often feels like *the* course for many students, especially in online settings. Students use the LMS to interact with the course in many ways, including uploading assignments, having online discussions, and reading course material.

Some LMSs offer a native badging system that allows instructors to award badges from within a course. Typically, these native systems are not very robust and don't allow much customization. However, a specification within LMSs can be used to add more functionality, including a commercial badge platform. This specification is called Learning Tools Interoperability, or LTI, and it allows a creator to make a tool that operates within the LMS. Because LTI is standardized, it can work with and be integrated into any LMS. Many educational technology software companies have taken advantage of LTIs in order to integrate their products, tools, and features seamlessly into an LMS to improve the experience of students and instructors. Some examples of other products or tools that offer LTIs are LibGuides, Credo Instruct modules, and Piazza. As you may have guessed, there are now LTIs for using badges within an LMS. The advantage of an LTI is that it lets you harness the features and details of that badge platform within the LMS and does so seamlessly for the learner. It allows learners to earn the badges from inside the LMS or "course" without having to navigate to and within another system. It also allows the instructor to track students' work and automatically report their grades or, in the case of badges, their achievements within the LMS.

Learning Pathways

In 2018, the badge platform Badgr released Badgr Pathways, a tool offering learners the ability to pull together various digital credentials, stack them, package them, and display the overall learning pathway for themselves and others. It takes the unbundling of learning a step further and allows users to gather credentials in ways that meet their needs or the demands of the company or industry to which they were applying.[5]

Badgr Pathways
https://pathways.badgr.io

Experiential Transcripts

Another development related to micro-credentials and part of the overall ecosystem that may help to drive adoption is experiential transcripts. As discussed earlier, traditional transcripts are lacking in details and often don't include types of learning outside traditional coursework. Job seekers may use tools like e-portfolios or social media to enhance their transcripts by showing alternative types of learning or engagement, such as service projects or independent research; however, in our experience, employers often cite the time needed to review these materials as one drawback to these tools. Additionally, activities listed on these platforms are typically not vetted or verified in any way. The experiential transcript, also called the comprehensive learning record, is one way that institutions are trying to marry the wide adoption and familiarity of transcripts along with the validation and authentication of open credentials.[6] Experiential transcripts are a way to pull together a student's learning that happens outside of a classroom into a more robust picture for both the student and the potential employer, evaluator, or supervisor. Types of experiences that could be included on an experiential transcript are study-abroad experiences, internships, service-learning projects, research activities or other engaged scholarship activities, and micro-credentials. Experiential transcripts share a lot of the same benefits as digital badges but offer them from a macro-credential level. They would provide a fuller picture of what learners have achieved and also would show learners how far they have come and what they have yet to do. Experiential transcripts could leverage the openness of other credentials, giving learners more ownership of their records. In addition, experiential transcripts could use open standards to make them interoperable with other systems or schools.

Additionally, experiential transcripts would shift some emphasis to other kinds of experiences and granular learning for all parties involved: students, schools, and employers. Thus, they would also allow libraries to become part of education in new and different ways. We know that employers value information literacy skills, and experiential transcripts would be another way to showcase these skills—a way that doesn't exist yet. Digital badges are already making inroads, but experiential transcripts would help to drive adoption of digital credentials and bring them into the mainstream. One of the biggest barriers facing experiential transcripts (and digital credentials too) is the paradigm shift, the biggest change being for institutions. Institutions would have to not only unbox the complexities of recording and verifying these types of activities, but also give learners a certain level of control over their own records. Moreover, there is no standard yet for experiential transcripts, but one would need to be implemented for the idea to take off.[7]

How Badges Are Being Used Today

Many of the developments outlined here and elsewhere in this report are related to a seemingly widening divide between employers and their perceptions of new graduates' skill compared to educators' perceptions of graduates' preparedness.[8] Closing this gap is one of the major drivers behind digital credentials and will require quite a bit of orchestration and coordination for them to see wider use. However, based on our own research, employers seem open to the idea of digital badges. We surveyed 114 employers from a variety of industries on whether they would consider digital badges as a criterion to determine a potential employee's credibility and knowledge. Of respondents, 60 percent said that they either would look at badges during the hiring process or would need more information but would consider it.[9] Below is a sampling of how digital badges are being used today in different spheres and what the next steps might be.

Education

Digital badges and micro-credentials are being used in all varieties of education from elementary schools through undergraduate and graduate education and the same benefits and principles apply at all levels. Students should be encouraged to cultivate and showcase granular skills beyond their report card, and digital badges allow for this kind of expansion. Fuller described in detail a workforce readiness digital badge initiative developed at Aurora Public Schools in Colorado. This program was designed to help students get internships and on-the-job experiences during high school and included badges for information literacy.[10] A digital badge program was also extended to students in grade and middle school to capture their learning of twenty-first-century skills at these grade levels.

In higher education, we also see a variety of uses for digital badges. In our program at Penn State, we are using them within undergraduate general education courses to deliver instruction around information literacy skills. In the health policy administration major at Penn State, digital badges are being used as a way to track learning outcomes that are tied to the program's accreditation. Other institutions are using badging systems as well, including Massachusetts Institute of Technology and Northeastern. We are also seeing badging used in massive open online courses (MOOCs) as a way to track a learner's progress.

Employers

Because many employers are seeing a disconnect between the actual knowledge and skills new graduates bring to the workforce and what they expect graduates to have, many employers have started issuing their own branded digital badges to fill the gap. In this scenario, workers earn digital credentials once they begin their employment as part of an onboarding program, when they learn a few new skills, or to help them get on track for a promotion or new job at the company. One of the earliest and fullest adopters of digital badges is IBM. From our own research, we found that the information technology industry was one of the early adopters of digital badges in general, and IBM, a leader in the IT industry, has fully embraced them.[11] In this program, IBM employees can find and participate in targeted training classes using the platform Coursera. Once a course is completed, employees complete a corresponding assessment, which allows them to claim their badge (using the Acclaim platform). IBM's badges are designed to help employees get skills in specific areas (e.g., data science or blockchain technology) so they can better complete projects, lead teams, and advance through their career.[12]

Employers are also using digital credentials for their employees' continuing education. In continuing education, teachers and other professionals are encouraged or required to extend their knowledge of the field, most typically by earning credits from an institution or professional organization. An employee must earn a certain number of credits to maintain good standing at the job or to be promoted to the next level. With this activity comes a lot of paperwork and verifying of information; therefore, it's a natural fit to take it to the next level by awarding badges. Using badges, learners can have access to all their records online in one place, and they have a way to share the records with their employer. The employer has a way to vet the veracity of the work or badge and hopefully streamline the administration of the badges. Some programs even offer rewards to learners after they have reached certain levels of experience, for example, getting to attend a special event.

As you might imagine, employers can see many opportunities using digital credentials that can make their employees smarter, more agile, and more empowered. By branding their own badges, they can incentivize learning in the strategic areas they identify as areas of growth. This use of badges also indicates to job seekers what the company values and is looking for going forward. Digital badges can also serve to streamline and clarify existing continuing education pathways that are well established in certain fields.

Libraries

Digital credentials in libraries are already being used in myriad ways from public to academic settings. In the example mentioned earlier, the Aurora Public School System used digital badges to document information literacy skills as one component of a larger system that focused on career readiness. Public libraries have also found digital badges as a means to reward patron achievements. Existing programs, such as summer reading, writing groups, and book clubs, are using badging. Badges are even being used to certify that a patron is able to use makerspace equipment. An early and now very robust program is the Chicago City of Learning, which seeks to give children and young adults a variety of experiences outside of school. These experiences and challenges are badged to give students a way to describe their learning journey. The Chicago Public Library is just one of many partners in this program, and it mainly features ways students can gain skills related to media, such as by learning to record or edit video.

In academic libraries, digital badges are primarily being employed to document information literacy skills—valued skills that too often go unrecognized in a formal way. The California State University at Fullerton has created a suite of interactive tutorials to guide students through what is probably their first foray into library research.[13] The State University of New York at Albany has developed a hierarchy of four related badges around the concept of metaliteracy, which is a component of information literacy.[14] As in public libraries, however, digital badges can also be used as a certification system for using specialized types of equipment, such as in makerspaces or virtual reality spaces.

As a resource for libraries interested in badges, aside from this report, the Association of College and Research Libraries (a division of the American Library Association) has a Digital Badges Interest Group that is open to anyone interested in the intersection of digital badges and libraries. The interest group's goal is to provide a means to discuss and exchange ideas related to digital credentials, libraries, and information literacy. This group holds regular online discussions and maintains an email discussion list and a blog with more information.[15]

Conclusion

As this chapter has demonstrated, the badging ecosystem is diverse and vast. There are new developments on the horizon and established ones that are being updated as this technology gains more adoption. The use of badges in different scenarios is also diverse and ever-changing at the moment. Hopefully after reading this chapter, you are imagining a few ways you can see digital badges fitting into your library's programs. In the remaining chapters, you will get more information about design considerations, implementation details, and ways to keep your program running smoothly.

Notes

1. Cinthya Ippoliti, "History of Micro-credentialing," in *Teaching with Digital Badges: Best Practices for Libraries*, ed. Kelsey O'Brien and Trudi E. Jacobson (Lanham, MD: Rowman and Littlefield, 2018), 3.
2. Carla Casilli and Daniel Hickey, "Transcending Conventional Credentialing and Assessment Paradigms with Information-Rich Digital Badges," *Information Society* 32, no. 2 (2016): 117, https://doi.org/10.1080/01972243.2016.1130500.
3. "About Open Badges," Open Badges website, accessed January 29, 2019, https://openbadges.org/about.
4. John Meerts, "Course Management Systems (CMS)," Educause Evolving Technologies Committee, October 20, 2003, 1, https://www.educause.edu/ir/library/pdf/DEC0302.pdf.
5. For an example of a Badgr Pathway, see Badger University, "Associate Degree: Biotechnology," January 28, 2019, https://pathways.badgr.io/public/pathway/5ad8eee4c9494851f4893554.
6. Educause Learning Institute, "The Evolution of the Transcript," *7 Things You Should Know About . . .* , January 2016, https://er.educause.edu/~/media/files/library/2016/1/eli7128-pdf.pdf?la=en.
7. Educause Learning Institute, "Evolution of the Transcript."
8. Casilli and Hickey, "Transcending Conventional Credentialing," 119.
9. Victoria Raish and Emily Rimland, "Employer Perceptions of Critical Information Literacy Skills and Digital Badges," *College and Research Libraries* 77, no. 1 (2016): 87–113, https://doi.org/10.5860/crl.77.1.87.
10. Amanda Rose Fuller, "Digital Badges in Action," in *Teaching with Digital Badges: Best Practices for Libraries*, ed. Kelsey O'Brien and Trudi E. Jacobson (Lanham, MD: Rowman and Littlefield, 2018), 64.
11. Raish and Rimland, "Employer Perceptions," 94.
12. "Badges," IBM Skills Gateway, accessed January 24, 2019, https://www-03.ibm.com/services/learning/ites.wss/zz/en?pageType=page&c=M425350C34234U21.
13. Lindsay O'Neill, "Pollak Library: Services and Collections," Pollak Library Spark Tutorials, *Instructional Design on a Shoestring* (blog), accessed January 29, 2019, http://lindsay-oneill.com/sparktutorials/servicescollections201819/story_html5.html?lms=1.
14. About page, Metaliteracy Badges website, accessed January 29, 2019, https://sites.google.com/view/metaliteracy/about.
15. "Digital Badges Interest Group," Association of College and Research Libraries, accessed January 29, 2019, https://acrl.libguides.com/c.php?g=549645&p=3773229.

Chapter 4

Six Roadblocks to Designing Digital Badges

Chris Gamrat and Brett Bixler*

In previous work, Gamrat, Zimmerman, Dudek, and Peck defined badges as "online representations of learning experiences and activities that tell a story about the learner's education and skills."[1] While at first glance this definition seems straightforward and badges appear easy to adopt, we offer that such may not be the case. In this chapter, we identify three internal challenges faced by badge creators and issuers and three external challenges faced by the larger education community. We argue that these six challenges present some of the largest barriers to the adoption of digital badges in education.

Three Internal Reasons

Digital badges require a significant degree of internal reflection about what they represent for an organization. Digital badges offer additional value and complexity because of the associated metadata and the transparent representation of the skills, abilities, and experiences valued by the badge issuer. For these reasons, the badge creators and issuers may invest significant time before they can reach a consensus on the badges that positively represent them and their institutions. Variations in badge design, assessment practices, and attention to the many details surrounding badge creation all contribute to this time factor.

Variation in Badge Design

Badges can range in size and scope. Badge design affords a great deal of flexibility regarding the scope of the task required to earn the badge. An organization could create badges that are awarded for attending a one-hour workshop or that completely align to an undergraduate or graduate degree. Digital badges' advantage is the capture of detailed information explaining the learning experience, what is required of the learner, and documented evidence of the completion of these requirements. Conventional wisdom might suggest that mapping a badge or suite of badges to something as large as a degree might be too complex, and also unnecessary because a series of data explaining the student's learning experience already exists—otherwise known as a transcript.

Since badges have value in different forms and represent different types of experiences, badge issuers may want to consider why they are issuing the badge, and badge earners may want to consider the number and types of badges they might share with a potential employer. Badge issuers should evaluate their goals for

* **Chris Gamrat** (PhD, Instructional Systems) is an Instructional Designer for the College of Information Sciences and Technology at Penn State University. He develops and supports the college's Master of Professional Studies degree programs. Gamrat completed his Ph.D. in 2018 in Learning, Design, and Technology from Penn State. He is currently focusing his research on personalized learning. **Brett Bixler** (PhD, Instructional Systems) is an Instructional Designer in the e-Learning Design Innovation Group (eLDIG), part of Penn State's Smeal College of Business. Bixler believes that engaging, motivating activities are at the heart of stellar learning experiences. In his current position, he works with the latest education technologies and learning theories to design engaging courses. Bixler is actively investigating the use of badging, educational games, and gamification for educational purposes, and works with various committees throughout the university to provide teaching and learning opportunities to Penn State students, faculty, and staff.

issuing badges, as this will help to determine the size and scope of the badges. For example, the badges may act as an additional layer of information that might supplement recognition that is already awarded, such as those associated with the completion of a class, degree, or certification program. Other badges could document skills and accomplishments beyond what an organization traditionally recognizes—for example, soft skills such as teamwork or problem solving.

Badges offer richer detail about achievements and experiences, which makes a badge a potentially valuable supplement to a résumé. However, in research conducted by Raish and Rimland, employers reported interest in reviewing badges within a limited scope, suggesting that the rules of résumés (brevity and conciseness) still apply.[2] Badge scope might require the consideration for how many criterion points to include in a badge—that is, how many steps or submitted artifacts are required to complete the badge. Digital badges may help learners to better elaborate on their learning experiences, but a badge author may want to consider this function of a badge and how it can help to translate the badge beyond its original context.

Badges Require Excellent Assessment Practices

As with any credential, various forms of badge assessments exist. Quizzes and written papers are often used for competency-based badges. Project-based badges may require more complex evidence of success, including portfolios or other tangible artifacts. Participation-based badges usually require the completion of a workshop, project, or course, where the assessment is not necessarily about the quality of a produced artifact but rather on social interaction and completion.[3] When used in concert, these assessment techniques may provide a rich perspective on what students know and can do.

Educators, administrators, and employers all want to ensure the claims students make about their earned credentials, certificates, or degrees are authentic. Rigorous assessments help to validate the claims about student achievement made by certificates and degrees in most educational environments, but often the assessment is hidden from the public. If badges are to be generally accepted as an alternative credential, then the assessment provided by the badge issuer must be visible to all and valid. As a badge ideally makes public the criteria and assessments for earning the badge and thus can expose weak assessment practices, badge creators and organizations are opened up to scrutiny and criticism.

The badge issuer ideally uses reliable and valid assessment instruments built into the badge criteria. Several statistical methods exist to ascertain the reliability and validity of multiple-choice quizzes. Badges that require portfolios or written materials may rely on a grading rubric that should be examined for intra-rater and inter-rater reliability.[4] If possible, badge issuers should include evidence of the reliability and validity of assessment instruments used in the badge to increase the badge's veracity. The quality of the assessment instruments used in badges is critical.

Complexities in Badge Design

The authors recently participated in an advisory committee helping interested faculty and staff through think-aloud exercises focused on the creation and implementation of digital badges. From this advisory role and our own experiences authoring badges, we can confidently say that the details of badge design can quickly become complicated. The concept of badging is easy to grasp. The processes needed to implement a badging system are complex. For example, just the instructional design considerations for badges are multifaceted, including aspects of content, assessment, and program scalability.[5] At first, implementing digital badges can seem easy, but addressing these complexities can be overwhelming. This may be especially true when the badge issuer is an organization with multiple stakeholders, inputs, and concerns.

As described above, the scope of a badge can be difficult to determine, but goal articulation will help to narrow what the badge means and what experience it is intended to recognize. To avoid becoming overwhelmed by the detailed questions presented by Gamrat, Bixler, and Raish, we recommend badge issuers start by considering primary reasoning for using digital badges.[6] Ahn, Pellicone, and Butler found that most researchers have approached digital badges with the goal of exploring student motivation, pedagogical considerations, or impacts to credentialing.[7] After determining the primary goal for creating and issuing badges, badge creators may be better able to consider content, assessment, relationships between digital badges, and program scalability.

Probably the most challenging detail for implementing a digital badging system is to determine how to scale the initiative. Badge ecosystems—the mechanisms needed to create, store, and issue badges—require a great deal of thought to conceptualize and significant resources (personnel and computer systems) to implement. Among the many questions to address are, Who handles the computing infrastructure? Who handles the uploading and storing of digital badges? Who updates the information?[8] Infrastructure questions add to the details of pedagogical and administrative questions, resulting in a balance among the three. Implementation and pedagogical strategies that work at the scale of a few dozen learners might be impossible with hundreds or thousands. Issuing digital badges in large numbers requires careful reflection, balancing high-quality assessment and grading timeliness. Decisions regarding implementing badges in large numbers likely cannot be made unilaterally, and achieving consensus can be a time-intensive process.

Three External Reasons

Badges present a value proposition at different levels of education: elementary and secondary education, higher education, and continuing education or professional development. Within informal and formal education, badges might be helpful in providing structure or motivation to students. However, when learners want to make use of their earned badges within a different context, such as a job application, potential barriers external to where the badges were earned arise.

Digital Badge Examination

Open badges were initially created by Mozilla as a way of establishing a set of standard metadata associated with digital badges. IMS Global picked up the open badges efforts from Mozilla and established the Open Badges 2.0 (OBv2) specifications in June 2018.[9] The specifications support the ability to transport digital badging information from system to system. The specifications on stored data are broad, so actual data from badge to badge can vary greatly while still following the Open Badges standard. This variability presents a challenge similar to that of comparing résumés or portfolios of work. While some large organizations have automated methods for streamlining résumé processing, manual review is still required to make decisions about what is valuable and how to compare across multiple and differing claims. To use an example, consider two applicants for a job, each claiming to have experience with multimedia production and both pointing to educational experiences to support the claim. Using digital badges or a course transcript presents similar comparison challenges. However, the digital badge for the experience has an advantage in that it fully describes the experience and provides evidence of the student's claim, whereas the transcript provides only the name of the course, the weight in course credits, and a letter grade received. The badge evidence is superior to the transcript but requires more effort to interpret. In an era where expert systems are used for initial comparison of job applicant credentials, digital badges will continue to require human appraisal.

Badges' Value Proposition

Badges form representations or claims of educational experiences that may or may not be valued by others. Similar to other educational currencies such as degrees or professional certifications, badges can offer a way of representing academic achievement through digital metadata. That is, for learners and employers, digital badges function as a mechanism to represent learning. We argue that digital badges, like other educational recognition, act as a currency to varying degrees in the three largest areas for learning: elementary and secondary learners preparing for postsecondary school, postsecondary learners preparing for jobs, and on-the-job learning for professional growth and advancement. In this chapter, we offer these three generalized scenarios for the adoption of badges as educational currency.

- **Elementary and secondary education.** Badges earned by learners in elementary and secondary schools document progress over time and motivate children to continue to learn and explore. In 2012, the Digital Media and Learning competition funded projects to design and implement badging systems. Many of these were for elementary and secondary student populations through 4-H and NASA, among many other projects.[10] More recently, Davis and Klein researched an afterschool science program for high school students.[11] This initiative offered the opportunity to use digital badges and explore student perception with this new credential. Some of the earliest educational research with digital badges in elementary and secondary contexts examined student engagement and motivation.[12] In these examples, the badges had value either in motivating students to engage with the content or in representing educational achievement for college applications.
- **Job preparation.** Digital badges are beginning to emerge as a tool for students to stand out in a crowd of applicants for a job. Purdue University and Brigham Young University have adopted a series of badges for their preservice teacher education programs.[13] Universities are also exploring the use of digital badges in a variety of areas outside the credit-bearing course. Penn State University Libraries offer a series of badges to recognize student learning in the area of information literacy.[14] In September 2018, Northeastern University and IBM announced a partnership in which Northeastern will accept badges offered by IBM to count toward college credit.[15]
- **Lifelong learning on the job.** Digital badges for tracking professional growth may help to encourage, track, and organize a lifetime of on-the-job learning. In 2012, Gamrat and colleagues developed and researched digital badges for teacher professional development.[16] This work helped to inform future efforts for the use of digital badges in independent professional development

settings.[17] Since then, other organizations have also adopted an approach to open-ended professional development in which the learner can choose what to learn and when. For example, IBM has provided a series of badges through a web resource, IBM Skills Gateway. The IBM Skills Gateway offers access to a library of technical and managerial modules and offers assessments upon completion of the content.

As indicated in the three generalized scenarios above, badge authors might view badges as metaphorical currency because the badges represent something they value. The currency metaphor must also pass the value test for both the primary and secondary audiences. That is, does the learner (primary audience) value the badge enough to put in the work to earn it, and do college admission offices and employers (secondary audience) see value in the badges that are earned? This is a significant external barrier to adoption as it requires significant numbers of people to agree on the value of a badge.

Buy-in for Badges

If badges are not deemed acceptable currency by the majority who interact with them, they will never be widely accepted. Badge earners need at least one badge in a given area for badges to be effective, but is there a true minimal number needed for badges to be accepted by earners, teachers, administrators, and employers? Although all these groups must be considered, this chapter examines buy-in at the individual level.

How are individual goals related to the acceptance of badges? At the individual level, goal setting is critical, and it is generally believed that grades and personal satisfaction are generally tied to academic goals. Although research is sparse here, the findings of one relevant study by Fanfarelli and McDaniel indicated the number of badges earned seems to correlate with a higher final grade for undergraduate males but not females. However, the authors infer that women may derive greater satisfaction from a badging system and earning badges than men.[18]

Research by Denny discovered a correlation between the number of times individuals viewed information about badges (possible goal setting and confirmation) and the number of badges collected.[19] The mechanisms that prompted individuals to view badge information seemed to play a role in the number of views. It must be noted that this was a study limited to badges collected on a single platform, not about badges collected over multiple platforms or offerings, making generalizations difficult. While these findings are preliminary and more research is needed in this area, it may be that the importance of the number of badges earned varies from individual to individual, and also from group to group. Mechanisms prompting students to view badges may contribute to the perception of the importance of badges at the individual level.

The structure of the goals within a suite of badges may also contribute to the acceptance and adoption of badges by the individual. Conceptualizing badge creation with proximal and distal goals may assist in the development of a suite of badges. The learner sees an immediate need to complete proximal goals—also called subgoals—and their value is clear to the learner. Distal goals are less urgent, and their value may be less clear.[20] A suite of badges, each with a small focus that contributes to a larger goal, is used in some programs, such as the Penn State Information Literacy Badge, and may be one method of creating the critical mass needed for a suite of badges.[21] The Penn State Information Literacy Badge consists of ten sub-badges that can be used to earn three "meta badges." If students earn the three meta badges, they can earn the overall "über badge," indicating they have successfully earned all the badges in the suite. The sub-badges here relate to proximal goals, such as "Refining Your Search," and the "Savvy Searcher" meta badge provides the distal goal.

Conclusion

Many educational institutions have not broadly implemented digital badges. Variations in badge design, evidence provided, the potential exposure of substandard assessments, complex support structures for badges, the variable value of badges, and buy-in by potential stakeholders all contribute to a slow pace of adoption. While it is possible from a technical standpoint to author and award digital badges, it is likely that the reasons outlined above are some of the major hurdles delaying implementing large-scale efforts with digital badges. We hope that the sections above offer the reader perspective on the challenges for adoption and some ideas on how they may be mitigated.

Notes

1. Christopher Gamrat, Heather T. Zimmerman, Jaclyn Dudek, and Kyle Peck, "Personalized Workplace Learning: An Exploratory Study on Digital Badging within a Teacher Professional Development Program," *British Journal of Educational Technology* 45, no. 6 (November 2014): 1136, https://doi.org/10.1111/bjet.12200.
2. Victoria Raish and Emily Rimland, "Employer Perceptions of Critical Information Literacy Skills and Digital Badges," *College and Research Libraries* 77, no. 1 (2016): 87–113, https://doi.org/10.5860/crl.77.1.87.
3. Daniel T. Hickey and James E. Willis III, "Where

Open Badges Appear to Work Better: Findings from the Design Principles Documentation Project," Center for Research on Learning and Technology, Indiana University, May 1, 2017.

4. Anders Jonsson and Gunilla Svingby, "The Use of Scoring Rubrics: Reliability, Validity and Educational Consequences," *Educational Research Review* 2, no. 2 (2007): 130–44, https://doi.org/10.1016/j.edurev.2007.05.002.
5. Christopher Gamrat, Brett Bixler, and Victoria Raish, "Instructional Design Considerations for Digital Badges," in *Digital Badges in Education: Trends, Issues, and Cases*, ed. Lin Y. Muilenburg and Zane L. Berge (New York: Routledge, 2016), 71–81, https://doi.org/10.4324/9781315718569.
6. Gamrat, Bixler, and Raish, "Instructional Design Considerations for Digital Badges."
7. June Ahn, Anthony Pellicone, and Brian S. Butler, "Open Badges for Education: What Are the Implications at the Intersection of Open Systems and Badging?" *Research in Learning Technology* 22 (2014), https://doi.org/10.3402/rlt.v22.23563.
8. John C. Foster, "The Promise of Digital Badges," *Techniques: Connecting Education and Careers* 88, no. 8 (November/December 2013): 31–34.
9. "Open Badges 2.0 (OBv2)," IMS Global Learning Consortium, accessed January 28, 2019, https://www.imsglobal.org/activity/digital-badges.
10. Daniel T. Hickey, Nate Otto, Rebecca Itow, Katerina Schenke, Cathy Tran, and Christine Chow, "Badges Design Principles Documentation Project: Interim Report January 2014 Update," Center for Research on Learning and Technology, Indiana University, January 2014, http://dpdproject.info/files/2014/05/DPD-interim-report-v4-january.pdf.
11. Katie Davis and Eve Klein, "Investigating High School Students' Perceptions of Digital Badges in Afterschool Learning," CHI '15: *Proceedings of the 33rd Annual ACM Conference on Human Factors in Computing Systems* (New York: ACM, 2015), 4043–46, https://doi.org/10.1145/2702123.2702413.
12. Samuel Abramovich, Christian Schunn, and Ross Mitsuo Higashi, "Are Badges Useful in Education? It Depends upon the Type of Badge and Expertise of Learner," *Educational Technology Research and Development* 61, no. 2 (April 2013): 217–32, https://doi.org/10.1007/s11423-013-9289-2.
13. Timothy Newby, Casey Wright, Erin Besser, and Elizabeth Beese, "Passport to Creating and Issuing Digital Instructional Badges," in *Foundations of Digital Badges and Micro-credentials: Demonstrating and Recognizing Knowledge and Competencies*, ed. Dirk Ifenthaler, Nicole Bellin-Mularski, and Dana-Kristin Mah (Cham, Switzerland: Springer International, 2016), 179–201.
14. Emily Rimland and Victoria Raish, "Design Principles for Digital Badges Used in Libraries," *Journal of Electronic Resources Librarianship* 29, no. 4 (2017): 211–20, https://doi.org/10.1080/1941126X.2017.1378540; Daniel L. Randall, J. Buckley Harrison, and Richard E. West, "Giving Credit Where Credit Is Due: Designing Open Badges for a Technology Integration Course," *TechTrends* 57, no. 6 (November 2013): 88–95, https://doi.org/10.1007/s11528-013-0706-5.
15. News@Northeastern, "Northeastern University and IBM Partnership First to Turn Digital Badges into Academic Credentials for Learners Worldwide," news release, September 25, 2017, https://news.northeastern.edu/2017/09/25/northeastern-university-and-ibm-partnership-first-to-turn-digital-badges-into-academic-credentials-for-learners-worldwide.
16. Gamrat et al., "Personalized Workplace Learning."
17. Christopher Gamrat and Heather T. Zimmerman, "Teacher Learning Journeys: A Design Case Study of a Learner-Centered Stem Digital Badging System," in *Digital Badges in Education: Trends, Issues, and Cases*, ed. Lin Y. Muilenburg and Zane L. Berge (New York: Routledge, 2016), 215–25, https://doi.org/10.4324/9781315718569.
18. Joseph R. Fanfarelli and Rudy McDaniel, "Exploring Digital Badges in University Courses: Relationships between Quantity, Engagement, and Performance," *Online Learning* 21, no. 2 (2017), https://doi.org/10.24059/olj.v21i2.1007.
19. Paul Denny, "The Effect of Virtual Achievements on Student Engagement," in *Proceedings of the SIGCHI Conference on Human Factors in Computing Systems* (New York: ACM, 2013), 763–72.
20. Zui Cheng, Sunnie Lee Watson, and Timothy James Newby, "Goal Setting and Open Digital Badges in Higher Education," *TechTrends* 62, no. 2 (March 2018): 190, https://doi.org/10.1007/s11528-018-0249-x.
21. Rimland and Raish, "Design Principles for Digital Badges."

Chapter 5

Collaborations and Partnerships

Emily Rimland and Victoria Raish

Collaborations and partnerships are critical to the success of many library instruction efforts. This is true at Penn State, where we do not have any sort of credit requirement for information literacy instruction. These collaborations create the potential for students to gain fluency in information and research literacy. These fluencies will help students be successful on their assignments.

To become information-literate, students need multiple opportunities to learn content through repeated and varied exposure.[1] Any information literacy integration that occurs should connect in meaningful ways to other learning the student is experiencing.[2] Such connections provide an opportunity for impactful information literacy instruction.

One of the large advantages of digital badges when it comes to partnerships in curriculum implementation is that they are micro-learning moments with chunked content. Each individual learning segment is on a small and easily defined scale, and the learning within that scale is chunked into digestible pieces of information for the learners. This learning design leads to flexibility in digital badge integration. A class can choose simply to use one or two badges; a program can use many badges; or badges can be used in both formal and informal learning environments. In this chapter, we'll look at the possible options for digital badge implementation.

Learning Environments

The growth of information and technology means that now, more than ever, students have the capability to learn virtually anything at any time. Universities are trying to capture this learning through the growth of student engagement.[3] Learning happens in both formal and informal learning environments, inside and outside of the classroom. Traditional records of learning, such as the transcript, are not adequately capturing and representing all of the knowledge that students are gaining. The currency of knowledge is changing in response to the evolving workforce and technological advances. Digital badges hold the potential to capture learning in all sorts of learning environments and settings. They give students the power to control visual representations of their learning, including privacy and sharing features. Digital badges, as part of the experiential learning record, is one way that learners can collect and curate learning from multiple learning environments.

Formal Learning Environments

Formal learning environments are those in which the content to be learned is in the control of the instructor or facilitator rather than the student. Common formal learning environments include classrooms or continuing education courses. The most frequently used currency in formal learning environments is a grade. However, a certificate or other measure may also be used, such as with CPR training or teacher workshops.

Some possible use cases of digital badges in formal learning environments include

- collaborating with an instructor of record
- serving as the instructor of record
- staff professional development
- conferences and other workshops

When digital badges are used in formal learning environments, there are some necessary considerations. The badges should be tied to other learning experiences within that formal learning environment. This makes them authentic and connected to the overall flow of learning. They also need to be at a level of value that makes sense in relation to the other work completed in that formal learning environment. If being used in the classroom, they could count for a grade or be combined into an overall participation grade. The points awarded to the badge should be consistent with other activities in the class. Very clear instructions should be provided to students so that they know exactly what they need to do to earn the digital badge.

It is easy for the instructor of record to decide when badges should be earned and for what point value. If library digital badges are being used in a collaborative partnership with another instructor, then conversations need to be had between the instructor and the librarian to determine when the digital badges will be offered to students, how long students will be given to earn a badge, and how the instructor will be provided with reports or evidence that a student has earned the badge.

Semiformal Learning Environments

Semiformal learning environments have aspects of both formal and informal learning. Learners self-elect to participate in such environments, and this learning environment is not connected to the student's official transcript. At the same time, a facilitator, leader, or instructor is associated with the learning environment.

Some possible use cases of digital badges in semiformal learning environments include

- a student group or organization
- student employees who participate voluntarily
- an independent study or internship

When digital badges are used in semiformal learning environments, it is important to offer flexibility in earning the badges and to connect them to the overall learning environment. There should be more autonomy from students in a semiformal learning environment because they are electing to participate in the activities. The badges should be designed with students' voluntary participation in mind. The activities and the assignments in the badges need to be relevant to whatever the student is applying in the semiformal learning environment. The due dates and rigid structure that guides the integration of badges in the formal learning environment will be more relaxed in this space.

For a successful badge implementation in the semiformal learning environment, it is essential that students clearly understand why they should earn the badge and the potential benefits of having this record of learning. Students are busy and try to participate in activities and complete things that offer them a rich experience. Without a clear purpose, badges risk becoming busy work or a piece of the learning that is not well integrated.

Informal Learning Environments

Informal learning environments should be primarily student-led. There might be a facilitator or mentor, but the decision-making power rests solely with the students. No longer are the students being told what they must learn, how they are going to learn, and why they need to learn. The students are choosing how to engage in learning. Informal learning environments could be group- or individual-based.

Some possible use cases of digital badges in informal learning environments include:

- student groups
- volunteer opportunities
- motivated individual student

For a successful badge implementation in informal learning environments, it is important to remember that it is entirely the student's choice whether to complete the badge. Sometimes, students might complete badges offered in classes on their own time because they see the intrinsic and extrinsic benefit. In the informal environment, it is quite challenging to force students to earn the badge.

Completion Rate

The MOOC phenomenon revealed a great deal about why people sign up for learning opportunities and why people drop out of learning activities.[4] This completion rate matters when it comes time to assess the success of your digital badge program. When evaluating the potential success of your digital badging program, consider the conditions associated with earning a badge. A class assignment where every student has to earn the badge would have a very high completion rate. If your badges are used in an optional setting, completion rates might not be the best metric on which to judge the success of your badge program. In all cases, the completion rate is only one data point in a pool of evidence and assessment data.

Personal Learning Spaces

Regardless of the type of learning environment in which students are earning badges, they need a place to store them as well as to document their other learning experiences. Students could potentially earn badges from many different locations or organizations. A centralized place to store all of these learning moments is critical. Students can create a holistic or experiential learning record that allows for documentation of the many activities they want to record and remember. The aggregation of different credentials means that there needs to be a central place in which to pull everything together. A record of an internship, service learning, and a badge are all records of learning not easily captured by the transcript.

IMS Global is an organization committed to creating a technical ecosystem that makes it possible for students to share their digital badges and other records of learning with relevant people, including possible employers or schools.

IMS Global
https://www.imsglobal.org

Residential Instruction

Despite the growth of online learning, many students are choosing to take residential courses and attend class in person. However, many of those classes have some aspect of their learning done online. They might have a syllabus in the learning management system, or maybe one class session has been replaced with an online activity.

When digital badges are used in the traditional classroom, they can be worked on during the class session. This creates an environment in which the instructor or librarian can scaffold and guide student work. The badge becomes one activity that students work on, and the class could be interrupted for a discussion or question. The badges could also be earned prior to the class by completing a traditional library one-shot. This would be considered a flipped classroom where the students are expected to participate in some academic activity prior to coming to the class session. This blended learning option tends to be popular with subject librarians who deeply value the opportunity to teach students face-to-face.

Online Instruction

Over 33 percent of students will have taken at least one online class in the 2016-2017 academic year. Many of these students are full-time online learners, as 15.4 percent have chosen to pursue their degree exclusively online. [5] Some are residential students who choose to take just a couple of online classes during their study. People choose online learning for a variety of reasons, but one of the most common is that their life schedule makes it very difficult for them to physically come to a campus for prescheduled class times. Online environments could be synchronous or asynchronous. Synchronous online classes have regularly scheduled seminar times with real-time communication. Asynchronous online classes never require students to meet at a specific time with the instructor. They use other methods for communication. Digital badges can be used in any online course.

When digital badges are used in the online classroom, students will be completing them from a distance, in their own time, and likely without the assistance of their classmates, their instructor, or a librarian. In this environment, the instructions for the digital badges must be as clear as possible because students will not have the opportunity to ask questions of their peers or instructor. Online students frequently work full-time jobs. For this reason, the due dates of activities and assignments should be on the weekend or later in the week so that all students have an opportunity to complete their classwork.

Formal Learning Badging Integrations

At Penn State, we have had the greatest success in integrating our badges within formal learning environments. We have utilized our existing partnerships with traditional curriculum partners, including English and communications programs, when starting these integrations. Our digital badges have been used in more than ten different courses and multiple sections of some of those courses. Implementation of digital badges in formal learning environments can happen within courses, within programs, or as standalone projects.

Within Courses

When a digital badge is integrated into a course, you need to decide on how many and which badges will be earned in the course. These decisions should be influenced by the overall workload of the course and how much time has been given to earn the digital badges. A well-designed digital badge takes time to earn. Within an individual course, this tends to be a time where less is more. Strategically choosing one or two badges provides a better overall experience than trying to fit all of your digital badges into one semester.

A badge should be earned shortly before starting a research assignment or before the librarian will teach the class in the event of a flipped classroom. This scheduling makes the badge more impactful and allows students to immediately apply the information and research skills that they learned through the digital badge. If badges are being earned in an individual course, then integrating the badge into the learning environment should be discussed with the instructor, as well as the instructional designer if one is involved in the course design. Important components of the conversation include which badges will be earned, at what point in the semester, the expected time line for returning the student work, and any sort of assessments you will complete after the students finish the digital badges.

Within Programs

Depending on the design of your digital badges, you might find that the ideal integration will be at the program level. This is especially true if you have developed some sort of hierarchical structure around the badges or conducted some mapping of learning objectives around the badges. In this instance, students would earn badges in certain classes over the entire span of the program. Students might earn one or two badges in these classes, and at the end of the program, they would have also completed your digital badge program.

At Penn State, our badges are designed to align with a program. We have lower-level badges that are grouped into larger categories. These categories are questioning information, searching, and organizing information, which are then located under the top badge, known as an über badge. This badge is a summative assessment of skills and requires students to synthesize and integrate all the skills they learned in the individual badges.

Program-level integration should be discussed with the program director, assistant dean, or teaching lead. The program point of contact depends on the organization of the program that you are partnering with. These are more complicated questions that require a higher and more complex level of buy-in, support of multiple faculty members, and a robust curriculum mapping. Badges must be associated with one course or multiple courses, learning pathways need to be built in, and students need to be made aware of these requirements at the beginning of their program so that they know what is expected of them and prepare accordingly.

Stand-Alone

The final way that digital badges could be used is in a stand-alone format without being tied to a course. This would occur when a student self-selects to complete a series of badges on their own time. As you might have guessed, this is the least common way that badges at Penn State are earned, but it does happen. When thinking about the implementation of badges for individual students not tied to a class, it is important to make sure that the student badge submissions are reviewed promptly. Depending on the structure of your badge system, it is possible that individual responses would get prioritized below those submitted by someone in a class or other group.

Semiformal and Informal Learning Badge Integrations

There is a lot of flexibility when considering how badges could be integrated into semiformal and informal environments. They could be offered to student employees of the library, or perhaps students participating in an undergraduate research exhibition could complete badges if they identified a need to improve their independent research skills.

If you decide to offer badges in this way, create a group and provide optional training to the individuals who will be working on the badges. The badges should still be tied to broader learning goals, but need not be tied to any formal curriculum. For example, suppose you are working on a badge for a club that has a goal of producing information to help other students determine the credibility of social media posts. Then your badge on media bias is connected to the broader goals of that student club.

In semiformal or informal learning environments, you should anticipate a lower completion rate as learners are choosing to complete the badges. Some may start and never finish, and others might not start at all. You should prepare for the maximum number of learners to complete the badges so that the initiative is sustainable. The number of potential earners should influence your design and enrollment limit for the badges. It is an individual decision how your badges should be designed and offered. If your badges are multiple-choice or otherwise scored by an automatic assessment, then they could be scaled to many learners or courses. If your badges require manual evaluation by a librarian, then it takes approximately three to five hours to evaluate one badge with an average number of five steps for twenty-five to thirty learners. There are always tradeoffs to be made in instructional design. If you want to see students' thought process, then text responses are ideal. If this articulation of thought is not as important to your goals, then you can use more automatically graded assessments. You can also use a blend of auto-graded and manual evaluations.

Another decision that needs to be made when integrating badges is where they will be located. Learners could be earning the badges either inside or outside the learning management system (LMS).

Badges can be offered directly through an LMS using learning technology interoperability. Some

LMSs might have badges offered as a gamification feature. These badges are not the same as open badges with the metadata and technical standards embedded. Badge systems including Badgr and Credly can be integrated into the LMS.

If learners are earning the badges in the LMS, the badges can be connected to the gradebook with the ability for both students and instructors to see student work without ever leaving the system. The badges still exist outside of the LMS, but they have functionality in the LMS. The advantages of placing the badges in the LMS include

- easy integration for students who are used to working in this environment,
- easy discovery of badges assigned,
- no need to move to an external system, and
- seamless connection with the gradebook.

There are also disadvantages to placing the badges in the LMS; they are the inverse of the advantages of earning the badges outside of the LMS, which are listed below.

Earning badges outside of the LMS means that learners need to go to the badging website and locate the badges they are supposed to be completing. The advantages of presenting the badges outside of the LMS include the following:

- Anyone is able to earn the badges without needing an access account.
- Learners can explore other badges and have access to the full system.
- People who are not familiar with the LMS have to learn only one system when going directly to the badge system.

This decision about working inside or outside the LMS does not have to be wholly one choice or the other. For example, if you are partnering with a formal course for one set of badges, you could use LTI (discussed in chapter 3) to place those in the LMS while at the same time partnering with an informal learning group like an undergraduate research lab where they earn badges outside of the LMS.

Completion Models

The final choice to make when integrating the badges into a learning environment is to decide if the badges will be required, recommended, or optional. This decision depends on the purpose of the badges and the goals of the integration. Remember that optional badges are likely to have the lowest completion rate while required badges will have the highest.

Required

A required badge means that the students are being made to complete the badge in exchange for some sort of credit. This could be a letter grade, participation credit, or as a prerequisite to another activity. These badges will normally require due dates and review of the evidence submitted by students in the badges in designated time lines.

Recommended

Recommended badges are those that learners are strongly encouraged but not required to complete. An example of recommended badges is a badging program at Penn State called The Library Connection. It is a series of four badges that every English composition distance student has the opportunity to complete. There is no requirement to complete them and no penalty for not completing the badges. This option works well when an academic department wants to partner on your badges but does not have a place to add another required activity.

Optional

The option "optional" is self-explanatory. Learners are given the option of whether they want to complete the badges or not. This type of badge will normally have the lowest completion rate. The learner who has the option of completing a badge or not needs to clearly understand its benefits.

Conclusion

Making the decision to partner and implement badges in a variety of learning environments requires a high degree of collaboration and outreach. There are many decisions to make, but the fundamental characteristic of any successful implementation is open and clear communication. This might mean negotiating and compromising so that the implementation is successful for all parties, but as long as you identify the minimum requirements you want out of an implementation, then these conversations can be successful. Even with a single implementation when you are the course instructor, it requires collaboration with other possible badge users, evaluators, and students. A common challenge that you might have in partnerships and collaborations is that some people are turned off by the term *digital badge*. In these situations, the word *micro-credential* can open ears that would otherwise be closed. That being said, the metadata that is unique to digital badges provides an assessment-rich environment that would otherwise not be present.

Notes

1. National Reading Council, *How People Learn: Brain, Mind, Experience, and School*, expanded ed. (Washington, DC: National Academic Press, 2000), https://doi.org/10.17226/9853.
2. Linda Darling-Hammond and Jon Snyder, "Authentic Assessment of Teaching in Context," *Teaching and Teacher Education* 16, no. 5–6 (July 2000): 523–45, https://doi.org/10.1016/S0742-051X(00)00015-9.
3. George D. Kuh, "Assessing What Really Matters to Student Learning inside the National Survey of Student Engagement," *Change: The Magazine of Higher Learning* 33, no. 3 (2001): 10–17.
4. Katy Jordan, "Massive Open Online Course Completion Rates Revisited: Assessment, Length and Attrition," *International Review of Research in Open and Distributed Learning* 16, no. 3 (June 2015): 341–58.
5. Doug Lederman, "Who Is Studying Online (and Where)," *Inside Higher Ed,* November 7, 2018, https://www.insidehighered.com/digital-learning/article/2018/11/07/new-data-online-enrollments-grow-and-share-overall-enrollment.

Chapter 6

Deployment and Sustainability

Emily Rimland and Victoria Raish

Once you have your badges designed, partnerships secured, and a path forward, you may be ready to launch your program. What follows are considerations for the deployment of your digital badges as well as for keeping the program sustainable and manageable. Some of these ideas may affect the learning design of your badges and cause you to alter your original designs, but now is the time to make these fixes before unleashing your badges out into the wild! Other details you probably won't be able to anticipate until you see student responses and get a sense for the "flow" of the badge evaluation process. Nonetheless, these considerations are meant to help you head off some of the major pitfalls as well as give you some ideas for the next steps to take.

Deployment

As with other new initiatives and programs libraries offer, a tried-and-true way to launch one is using a pilot. A small group of users who can authentically work through your digital badge program; find and report any bugs, glitches, or confusing wording; and successfully navigate to the right places will be extremely helpful. A pilot will also give you a sense of what the evaluation workload will look like and how much time and effort will truly be needed by evaluators. This pilot phase is also good for collecting and incorporating any user experience feedback on the design of the badges and navigation of the digital badge platform. At Penn State, we have a homegrown badging platform and a working relationship with the developers, who are always open to user experience feedback to make the platform better. If you are using a commercial badging platform, consider submitting help-desk tickets or feedback about your issues—many vendors are receptive to this kind of feedback and incorporate fixes and upgrades regularly. For a pilot, we recommend finding a partner who is an early adopter or a champion of the library or information literacy. By working with someone who is enthusiastic and supportive of the process of launching a new technology or of the library's goals, you will have a smoother rollout. Additionally, a partner who is a supporter will tell all their friends about the program, helping you spread the word. Not to put too fine a point on it, having a smooth rollout and enthusiastic partners is critical to the success of the deployment of your badge program. Therefore, the pilot is key to getting your program off the ground. We also highly recommend evaluation or grading rubrics. What follows are the most common types of submissions for badge steps, their pros and cons, and evaluation considerations. Since each badge platform operates differently, take the variations your platform has into consideration.

Free-Text Responses

Free-text response submissions are simply written answers by learners that will be read and verified by evaluators. In this scenario, the learner is responding with original ideas to a question or prompt in the badge step's instructions, and the response could be in list or paragraph form. In the embryonic days of our own badge platform, this was one of only three types of submissions that were offered, and thus we used it (and still do) for many of our badge steps. An example screenshot from our own sets of badges is shown in figure 6.1; it includes the grading criteria (aka rubric), student response, and sample reply using the Penn State system. Additionally, some other open-ended questions and prompts from our badges are listed below.

Example prompts for free-text responses:

- "For this step, type in your research question and come up with a few keywords for your particular research topic and list them in the box below. Try to create three keywords." (For a badge on developing a research question)
- "Do you now feel more comfortable evaluating a website? Do you feel that you could evaluate information on your own after completing this badge? Would you change anything about this activity? Does evaluating a website remain confusing for you or is it clearer now? Please include a short paragraph (4–5 sentences) or the equivalent web 2.0 technology creation in the textbox." (A final reflection for a badge about evaluating web credibility)
- "Your evidence for this step is to write 2–3 sentences on what part of the librarians' job surprised you the most and a question that you might have as a result of viewing the video. Is there a librarian whose job you want to learn more about? Is there a service these librarians provide that surprised you? We want to know what you thought of the video." (From a badge introducing our virtual reference service to undergraduates)

Additionally, in this type of submission, you can use third-party online tools to let students get more creative. For example, students may prefer to create a quick slide show in Google Slides or a VoiceThread response. Using the evidence box, students can simply enter a URL to their web-based multimedia response, which evaluators can view on that website (although students should be reminded to make any work open, at least to the reviewers) and then respond as usual via the badging platform.

VoiceThread
https://voicethread.com

Hands down, one of the pros of the free-text response submissions is the insights into the learner's mind that you see when reviewing the evidence. By having open-ended questions, the evaluator gets valuable insight into what the learner is thinking (see figure 6.1). A related benefit is that text responses help you keep a finger on the pulse of what is popular with students in terms of research topics, their values, and where they have trouble or ease with learning the content of the badges. Below are a few collected anonymous responses that give a sense of the insights we tend to see when evaluating student work. For the librarian who is accustomed to teaching one-shots and having only surface-level interactions with students, evaluating these responses can be eye-opening and very informative.

- "I think this badge will help me with practically every paper I write in the future. Research is such a big part of Psychology."
- "At first the keywords I was using were not very effective as I was not getting many helpful sources. Once I learned how to broaden and narrow my keywords, I found that my research skills improved when I was exposed to much more helpful information."
- "This badge activity has caused me [to] reexamine my own method of how I select keywords, and it has increased my understanding of investigating topics for research."
- "I have used scholarly articles for the research in my papers for the past 3 years, but this helped me identify a few new differences between scholarly and popular articles. I was not aware that popular articles did not cite their information, so if I have a questionable source, I can use this idea to find out whether or not it is scholarly. Truthfully, I wish I would have been given this badge when I was a freshman. Honestly, I had no idea there was a difference between scholarly and popular articles then, and this would have helped tremendously."

Conversely, the main drawback of evaluating text responses by students is the time-intensive nature of the process. As one might imagine, if you deploy your badges to lots of people who are actively engaged with the content, you would be quickly inundated with responses and evaluating lengthy text responses could get cumbersome. Some solutions for this are listed in the sustainability section below.

Document Uploads

The document upload submission type is one where the learner attaches a file or document in the badging platform for the evaluator to review. This type of response could be an extension of the text response and would allow the learner to use word processing software to make a more formal document and include things like tables or charts. It would also be appropriate for a capstone type project that might be a research paper, which would be much longer than a simple response to a question. Additionally, by using this type of response, other types of files could be added, such as spreadsheets or slides, so again, a return to your badge design and determining what kinds of outcomes you'd like to see from the learners will help you decide on the format to fit the badge.

This submission type has benefits and drawbacks similar to those of the free-text response. As an evaluator, you'd be able to see learners' work directly and

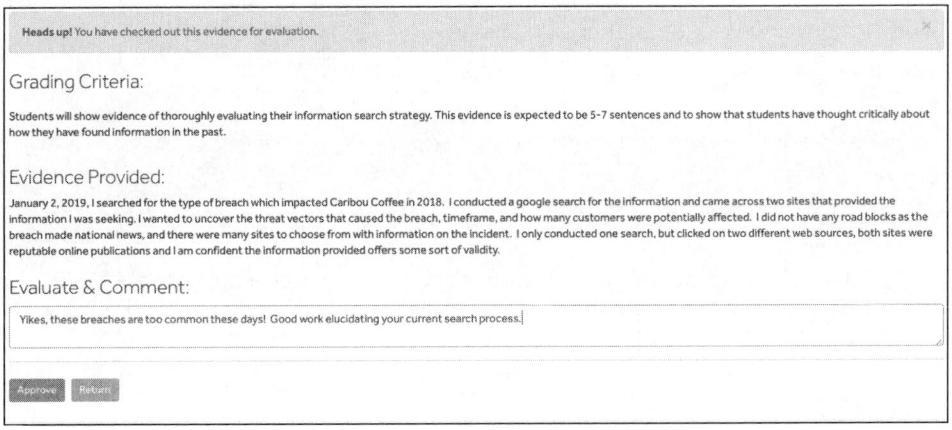

Figure 6.1
A screenshot of Penn State's badging platform showing the grading criteria for the evaluator, a student's response to a prompt (evidence), and a follow-up answer by an evaluator.

gain insights from seeing their evidence. This format allows the learners to use other software or applications to expand the formats for their work and allows more creativity than just text. On the other hand, adding a layer of complexity with an upload option can make evaluation time even longer or more intense. Again, the number of submissions you expect would have a huge implication for the workload. Reviewing research papers for five students would be quite different from papers for 100 students. Another aspect to consider is the variety of file types learners might potentially upload. Speaking from experience, unless students are explicitly told what types of file format to upload, you might find yourself with some submitted files that are not platform-agnostic—for example, .pages files that cannot be read on a Windows machine. Also, depending on your badge platform and computer environment, downloading, opening, and viewing files may quickly become a tedious process. Again, this workflow can be significantly different depending on the number of the responses in your queue.

Auto-graded Quizzes

Most badging platforms offer a quizzing tool that can be used in badge steps as an assessment for learners' understanding of the content. In most cases, these quizzes are auto-graded within the platform based on the correct answer being input ahead of time by the designer. The most popular type is multiple-choice quiz questions, but true/false, matching, or ordering type questions might be options as well. This option is generally good for quick assessments, particularly formative assessments along the course of a badge where learners can self-check their own comprehension along the way. In the early days of our own badge platform development, auto-graded quizzes were not an option, so we didn't initially have any included. Today we have a sprinkled a few quizzes into our badges (see figure 6.2), but from an instructional design perspective, we feel they are not best for the designs where we focus on student articulation of their learning through reflection. In our student feedback about our digital badges, we sometimes have students offer suggestions that the badges should include more quizzes. One pro of this type of response is that students seem to like the familiar and often easy format of a quick quiz as opposed to writing a thoughtful response to a question. In fact, they occasionally suggest that more or all of the steps be quizzes. Additionally, in this format, it is difficult or impossible to respond to the student's work with personalized feedback. One pro of quizzes is that the step is graded immediately for the student and the evaluator. As an evaluator, you may be able to see the quiz answers either individually or in the aggregate so you can see where students have trouble. Conversely, depending on the platform, you may not be able to provide personalized feedback on quiz work. While it's tempting to make every step of a badge a quiz due to learners' preferences and ease of evaluation, we caution against this type of blanket approach to submissions. Quizzes are not an assessment that fits every type of learning, learner, or topic. Consider the design of the badge and what you would like students to learn. If the content requires critical thinking and articulation of knowledge, a quiz may not be the best fit. However, if the step is providing new information and facts about a topic, a quiz might be a good fit and provide some welcome variety over the course of a badge.

No Evidence or Optional Evidence

Occasionally, you may have a step that asks a learner to do some task or take note of information that is required as part of the learning journey but doesn't necessarily require that the learner submit evidence. In this case you could have a badge step where no evidence is required or the learner can submit evidence as an option. We have two examples of such a step from our own digital badge program (see figure

6.3 for one example). As an example of a badge step where no evidence is required, we ask students to review and bookmark a site for future reference but don't require that they submit evidence and take their word that they've done it. As an example of an optional evidence badge step in a badge about citations, we give students the option of submitting a citation to us for review and feedback. In this case, not all students submit something, which means we are addressing the students who are focused on learning the topic. Another use case for this type of evidence would be a reading you want students to complete but do not need them to respond to questions about it.

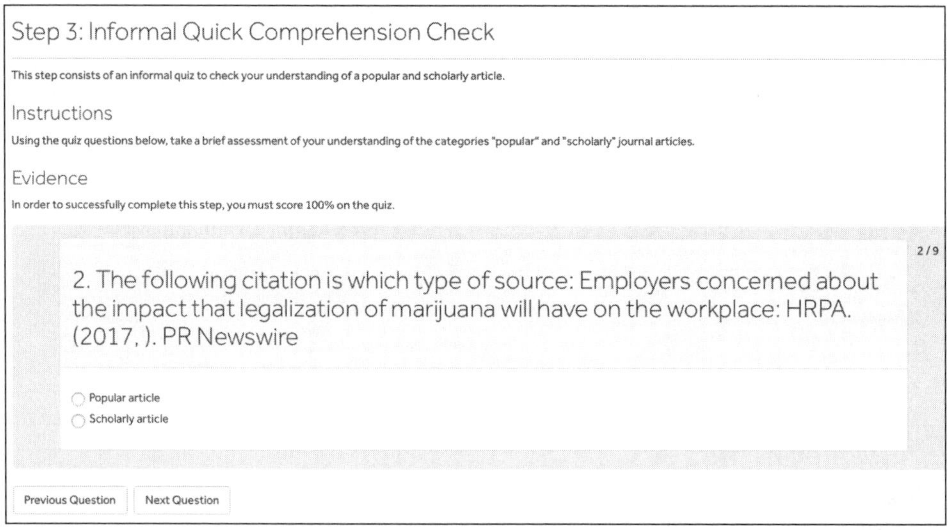

Figure 6.2
A screenshot of Penn State's badging platform showing a step using an auto-graded quiz.

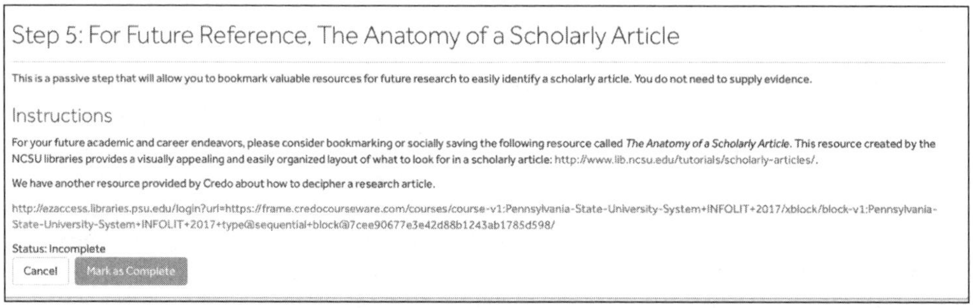

Figure 6.3
A screenshot of Penn State's badging platform showing a badge step that doesn't ask the learner to submit a response.

The benefits of having no or optional evidence required are that you can still place needed or supplemental materials into the design of the badge, but learners and graders both get a break from submitting and evaluating evidence. If you have a large number of learners working through a badge, this option can allow you to incorporate something that might be hard to test or reflect on without interrupting the flow of the badge. The obvious drawback to this approach is that you don't have explicit confirmation that the learner did the task, and you also don't have data or feedback about this particular step. This type of submission may not be the most common one for badges, but it can be useful and should be considered at times.

Sustainability

This section will cover some ideas to consider for your digital badge program to keep all of the different aspects working smoothly, your users' expectations managed, and your work sustainable. At Penn State, the question of scale is always looming large because having over 90,000 total students (online and residential) means that most classes we interact with are either large or have multiple sections. Any program we launch needs to have some built-in growing room if we want to build a program to have impact on larger groups or programs. If you aren't at a large institution like ours, you will still want to consider these suggestions for your own situation as they will help you plan for potential pain points ahead of time or at least be braced to deal with an issue should it arise.

Evaluation Time

Time needed for evaluation is one of the biggest sustainability issues we've faced and one area to definitely consider proactively. The design of your badges will impact not only the learners but also you and your colleagues. The amount of time it will take to evaluate the evidence that learners submit for their digital badge work is probably the biggest area that will affect you day to day. When considering the different types of responses outlined above, some types of responses clearly require more time and effort than others, with document uploads and text responses being the most time-intensive and auto-graded quizzes and no or optional responses being the least time-intensive. The learning theory driving our design was connectivism with a focus on placing resources in key moments within the learning experience. Therefore, we didn't want the majority of the student work to be auto-graded quizzes—rather, we wanted students to think critically and respond. One approach we've taken over time is to provide a mix of response types in each digital badge. Giving the learner a choice of ways to respond to questions in the digital badge helps as well. Also consider the type of response students will be articulating. Is it a reflection of their experiences where there isn't a "wrong" answer per se, or are you looking for a specific response? Due to the nature of the evidence, the first is easier to evaluate than the second, and this would be a factor in time required for evaluation.

As an evaluator, you become faster and more skilled the more responses you verify. Once you get a handle on what you are looking for in a response, you will be able to deftly identify a "good" response. In our own experience, we find that the large majority of students do the work appropriately and don't need multiple attempts to pass a step or earn a badge, which also helps to speed evaluations. As mentioned earlier, grading rubrics or criteria for evaluating responses will also help limit time needed for evaluating responses, especially text or multimedia responses.

Another way you can ease evaluation is to enlist your colleagues and crowdsource this aspect of your program. When our program started taking off and we were inundated with evidence to evaluate, we quickly found a few supporters who were willing to pitch in to help. That cadre of evaluators soon grew to over a dozen people and is the main way we've been able to expand our program. We've created an orientation and training curriculum for volunteer evaluators and put out a call twice a year to find new helpers. Once new evaluators are onboarded, we offer to co-evaluate with them until they feel secure responding to students and go at a pace they are comfortable with.

If you don't have many colleagues or helpers to draw upon, another way to keep your work manageable is to limit the number of participants completing badges. You can do this by making them optional, but if you want to see badges completed in their entirety or the badges are part of a scaffolded program, you'll want to make them mandatory, so limiting the number of people who can earn them may be the option you want to use. This method can make your program seem more exclusive while at the same time keeping your workload manageable. Additionally, it means you will be spending more time on each response and providing meaningful feedback, if that's how your badges are designed.

Artificial Intelligence

Aside from changes in staff support to manage a digital badge program, there's technology on the horizon that may help more in the future, one we've recently gotten to explore in detail—artificial intelligence (AI). While our crowdsourcing approach is a success, it is not likely to be sustainable at the current growth rate. The integration of digital badges changed our pedagogy by deepening the learning experience for the student and the teaching experience for the librarian. We didn't want to move away from the philosophy of providing personalized feedback in our digital badge designs, but at the same time wanted a way to automate parts of the process in order to make it more efficient. This is when we turned to AI.

The type of AI we are exploring, automated essay scoring (AES), is used to assess the quality, accuracy, and relevancy of natural language writing. Recent advances in machine learning (ML) have led to significant improvements in the accuracy of AES, and evaluation of student responses in micro-credentials is a natural application of this technology, yet an underexplored one, and certainly so within libraries. Our micro-credential data is well-suited to various ML techniques because we've had so much success with adoption, and thousands of responses are available in order to train an AI model.

Luckily, our institution was offered seed funding for AI-based projects, and we partnered with our I-School (College of Information Sciences and Technology) to develop an AI tool that integrates human and algorithmic capabilities. The AI gives students indicators as to whether their response is likely to be successfully scored and speeds the grader's response time so that personalized feedback will still be possible at scale. Through this process, we learned how challenging it is to integrate AI into an environment very concerned with data privacy and how integrating new technology into existing systems requires careful coordination.

Although the use of AI is on the rise and we've started to use it in our everyday lives, it is still a developing technology. It's important to remember that using a developing technology where student grades are potentially impacted is an area to especially tread lightly. With our experimentation with AI, we felt it was and will be critical to have a human in the loop throughout the process. However, we can clearly see how AI will have an effect on digital badges as well as other areas of libraries in the future.

Conclusion

It is our hope that with our own experiences in mind, you will have a clearer path forward with your own digital badge program and that by considering some of our challenges and ideas up front, you will be in a better place to be agile and responsive to your learners' needs so that you have a successful launch of your program.

Chapter 7

Assessment

Emily Rimland and Victoria Raish

The library world faces pressure to prove our worth or have some measurable impact. This situation has led to the growth of research trying to correlate libraries to improved academic performance or emphasizing the important role of libraries in the open educational resources movement. Fortunately, digital badges have evidence and other forms of assessment metadata baked into them. This technical standard is critically important to demonstrating the value of digital badges. In fact, this standard and the open badges framework are truly a tremendous strength of digital badges. Educause published an article in 2017 that analyzed the mismatch between the rhetoric and reality of digital badges.[1]

One of the most powerful aspects of a digital badge is that an open badge has "metadata fields that function as dynamic narratives of learning."[2] The badge ties together the learner story through the evidence with the approval of that evidence and validity of the badge apparent. While not all of the metadata fields need to be filled in every time, the more descriptive the data, the more searchable and findable the badge will be within the database and the better that the badge will be able to talk to other relevant systems. This chapter will explore assessment through three levels: within badges, across badge programs, and through badge ecosystems.

Assessment within Badges

Most of the assessment of individual badges comes from the evidence that is submitted as part of the steps of that badge. Evidence can be submitted in several different ways. Learners can take a short quiz demonstrating their knowledge, or they can upload a screenshot demonstrating something they did, take a video of their project, create a web-based object, upload a file, or enter a response in a textbox. The evidence that you choose to accept for your badges should primarily be driven by your learning outcomes and instructional design approach. Automated assessments are appropriate for some activities, while others are designed to have students externalize and articulate their thinking. There is value in both types of evidence, and each step of the badge could require a different type of evidence depending on what is required to complete that step of the badge.

While learning outcomes and design philosophy are absolutely a large part of deciding which evidence to accept, another factor to consider is scale and sustainability. Naturally, text-entry responses and file uploads will take longer to grade than an automated quiz. However, they also provide different insights into student learning. When designing a badge step, you should always ask if assessment of the step can be automated, and if not, why not.

When you have to think about economies of scale, there is always a balance between the ultimate type of activities you want students to apply their knowledge in and the available resources you have to evaluate that student work. For example, if you are going to be the only one administering the badge program, then having more automated assessments will make the badging program more sustainable. Just realize that, by creating automated assessments, you will be giving up the ability to read the thought process of every student who is completing the badge. Krajcik and Blumenfeld emphasize the importance of externalization and articulation of thinking that the learner is experiencing as they learn concepts to assess their formative understandings of a concept. [3]

Two examples from our work illustrate the decisions behind badge evidence types. To earn one of our badges, students select the citation style they would use in their field. We link out to a resource that lists the majority of citation styles and what fields tend to use it. While it is interesting to read comments, such as "I had no idea there were citation styles beyond APA or MLA," assessment of this step could be automated with a multiple-choice survey in which students select the citation style most closely related to their field.

In another step to earn a different badge, students create initial keywords and then narrow their focus based on the initial results received. Students enter in a textbox their initial keywords and search results, and then their narrowed keywords and search results. It would be nearly impossible to automate assessment of this step, as we want insight into the descriptors students are using for their specific topic. One way we could automate this step would be to choose a topic for students, create keyword searches, and then require students to select the best search. However, since our badges are designed to be meaningfully tied to assignments, we want students to choose a topic that interests them and that they are going to use in their course assignment. If this connection is not part of your instructional design, you could automate this step. The decision of what evidence to require in a badge is an intentional decision between assessment types and can be refined over time. You might start with the decision to automate the assessment of a step and then discover that seeing the articulation of thought in that step would be helpful.

The benefits of automated assessment are clear in that the badges are infinitely scalable and sustainable with very little manpower required on the part of the badge creators and evaluators. However, there are also constraints in the types of questions that can be asked in multiple-choice assessments and the level of learning that can be assessed. Textboxes and other creative entries allow for deep insight into student thinking around topics, but this evidence takes time to evaluate and limits the amount of scaling that can occur.

In order to assess the effectiveness and design of one badge, consider scheduling times to review comprehensive evidence submitted for that badge. Depending on the badge system you use, you should be able to pull evidence and analyze it to determine if there are any pain points or other areas where your badges are not producing desired results.

Assessment of Badge Programs

When you think about assessing badge programs, the level of assessment should move beyond individual badges to the overall quality and effectiveness of a complete program. To assess quality and effectiveness, it is helpful to create surveys or other measures of feedback that are given to key stakeholders. These stakeholders include students, instructors, and other librarians who might be assisting in the badge evaluation.

It is important to realize that if the survey is not required, the overall completion rate might be very low. Survey results should be considered in a holistic manner with any other evidence that points to the quality and effectiveness of the badge program. Take any survey results and combine them into a holistic approach of the quality and effectiveness of the badge program. Some other measures of assessment of the badging program are free text responses within the badges, comments from students, and overall completion numbers for the badges. When thinking about the program, it is also important to assess the overall process and technical logistics of earning the digital badges. If the user experience is clunky and not intuitive, then learners can get frustrated before they even begin working on the actual activities you have designed.

Assessment of Ecosystems

Badging ecosystems go beyond the individual badges and badge programs at one library. If your institution has a larger badging program, then that is an ecosystem that can be assessed. If not, the external digital badging world has large and connected ecosystems.

One of the biggest critiques of digital badges is that it is really hard to tell a valid and quality badge from a badge that has less evidence and fewer requirements.[4] This is a realistic concern, but efforts are being made to assess badging ecosystems. One of the most important developments is the use of BadgeRank by Badgr. This is a search engine that allows searching and ranking of badges. Theoretically, with mass adoption of this system, quality badges will rise to the top. It can also provide a way for employers to quickly check the validity and worth of a badge.

BadgeRank
https://badgerank.org

Another aspect of assessing the badging ecosystem is looking at the connection to social media platforms, such as LinkedIn, or to a learner's experiential learning record. This assessment could explore how often learners choose to push their badges to their social media accounts or how often employers view digital badges that have been pushed to LinkedIn.

We conducted a badging ecosystem assessment in a 2016 article for *College and Research Libraries* that explored the willingness of human resource professionals in ten distinct fields to accept digital badges as a form of evidence for students working on information literacy skills.[5] Other colleagues and researchers have also conducted research on badging ecosystems.[6]

Future Assessment Directions

Learning analytics are going to drive the future of much assessment, and digital badges are not immune to the use of learning analytics. The field of learning analytics is still very much in its infancy. However, the nature of digital badges means that a massive amount of data is being collected and stored. This data can be used to analyze the effectiveness of digital badges and digital badge ecosystems.

As mentioned in the previous chapter, another possible technology that might help with assessment and the entire badging ecosystem is artificial intelligence. This field is also in its infancy, but it has the potential to help scale badging programs and reduce the labor involved in creating and organizing badging systems.

Notes

1. Viktoria Strunk and James Willis, "Digital Badges and Learning Analytics Provide Differentiated Assessment Opportunities," *Educause Review*, February 13, 2017, https://er.educause.edu/articles/2017/2/digital-badges-and-learning-analytics-provide-differentiated-assessment-opportunities.
2. Strunk and Willis, "Digital Badges and Learning Analytics."
3. Joseph S. Krajcik and Phyllis C. Blumenfeld, "Project-Based Learning," in *Cambridge Handbook of the Learning Sciences*, ed. R. Keith Sawyer (New York: Cambridge University Press, 2006), 317–34, https://doi.org/10.1017/CBO9780511816833.020.
4. Troy Markowitz, "The Seven Deadly Sins of Digital Badging in Education," *Forbes*, September 16, 2018, https://www.forbes.com/sites/troymarkowitz/2018/09/16/the-seven-deadly-sins-of-digital-badging-in-education-making-badges-student-centered/#79cdb1670b8b.
5. Victoria Raish and Emily Rimland, "Employer Perceptions of Critical Information Literacy Skills and Digital Badges," *College and Research Libraries* 77, no. 1 (2016): 87–113, https://doi.org/10.5860/crl.77.1.87.
6. Nate Otto and Daniel T. Hickey, "Design Principles for Digital Badge Systems: A Comparative Method for Uncovering Lessons in Ecosystem Design," in *New Horizons in Web Based Learning ICWL 2014 International Workshops SPeL, PRASAE, IWMPL, OBIE, and KMEL, FET Tallinn, Estonia, August 14–17, 2014 Revised Selected Papers*, ed. Yiwei Cao, Terje Väljataga, Jeff K. T. Tang, Howard Leung, and Mart Laanpere (Cham, Switzerland: Springer International, 2014), 179–84, https://doi.org/10.1007/978-3-319-13296-9_20; James E. Willis, J. Quick, and Daniel Hickey, "Digital Badges and Ethics: The Uses of Individual Learning Data in Social Contexts," in *Proceedings of the 2nd International Workshop on Open Badges in Education co-located with the 5th International Learning Analytics and Knowledge Conference (LAK 2015), Poughkeepsie, NY, March 16, 2015* (New York: ACM, 2015), 41–45, https://dblp.org/db/conf/lak/obie2015.

Chapter 8

Conclusion

Emily Rimland and Victoria Raish

In this report, we provided a comprehensive deep dive into micro-credentials, digital badges, and related topics and technologies. At the beginning of the report, we listed some potential benefits of badges, such as data richness and access to education. As with any new technology, it should be noted that the list of benefits is not exhaustive, and they are sure to change as the badging ecosystem becomes more developed and robust. We mentioned a few of the key players in the current environment when it comes to badging platforms. These commercial vendors are just one aspect of digital badges, but as the vendor platforms become more feature-rich and integrated into things like our learning management systems, they may begin to play a larger role in the adoption rate and use of digital badges.

The adoption of digital badges was slower than many educators had anticipated, but this slowness is likely because of the paradigm shifts involved in such a big change and the orchestration between the different players: learners, educators, and employers. Implementing a digital badge system is complex and requires several decisions, partners, and actions. All of these factors can slow down the rate of adoption. Although technology seems to change quickly, the disruption to established systems can take quite a bit longer. Chapter 4 of this report discusses the design of digital badges and how design can either cause barriers or open doors for implementation. In our experience, design choices are extremely critical to the success of a digital badge program.

Equally critical are the collaborations and partnerships you potentially establish for your digital badge program. Finding earlier adopters or evangelists for your program is going to be key to developing a successful program as well. It is important to tie the badges into the larger context or learning environment. In addition, without providing a framework or larger structure for your badges to feed into, it will be hard for people to see their relevance. Thankfully, with the OBI, the open nature of badges has been baked in from the beginning, and thus there are a few built-in ways to share badges earned with a larger audience.

In later chapters, we dug into the details of deployment, sustainability, and assessment in the hopes of giving you some concrete considerations for your program before it was fully underway. Since much of this type of work may be new, it's helpful to think through some of the day-to-day concerns you might be dealing with to anticipate any issues. As we wrote Chapter 6: Deployment, implementing your program by way of a pilot is a recommended path forward with a digital badge program; however, a deep dive into the design of your badges and the larger system at the beginning of your work is potentially very beneficial, and we sought to discuss those details throughout this report.

It bears repeating that the badging ecosystem is complex and digital badges and micro-credentials are already causing ripples of disruption. The players involved have the potential to change the playbook for things like how job applicants get evaluated for jobs—by flipping the script and giving job seekers more control and power over the representation of their skills. Libraries have the power to be a partner in this disruption, which we believe has the potential to not only transform education and employment, but also showcase the power of information literacy as part of lifelong learning.

Notes

Library Technology REPORTS

Upcoming Issues	
May/June 55:4	**Librarians as Online Course Designers and Instructors** edited by Lucilia Santos Green
July 55:5	**Strategic and Intentional Integration of Technology in Library Instruction** edited by Heather Moorefield-Lang
August/ September 55:6	**Planning and Implementing a Sustainable Digital Preservation Program** by Erin Baucom